WHERE WE LIVE IS...
CREATIVE

For Fiona,
who seized every opportunity to wonder at the world.

Bosky Publishing Limited
Stockport
Greater Manchester

First Published in Great Britain 2025
© Bosky Publishing Limited
Author Emily Shore
Illustrations by Marion Lindsay

Emily Shore has asserted her right under the Copyright, Designs and Patents Act, 1988, to be identified as Author of this work.

All rights reserved. No part of this publication may be reproduced or transmitted in any form or by any means, electronic or mechanical, including photocopying, recording, or any information storage or retrieval system, without prior permission in writing from the publishers.

The author and publisher have made every effort to ensure that details were correct at the time of publication however we cannot accept any responsibility for changes in events and artworks beyond our control. We accept no responsibility or liability for the content or operation of websites which are not under our control. The examples of creativity in this book are a snapshot of creativity and not meant to be exhaustive but a set of relatable examples. The 'Where we live' series is copyright of Bosky Publishing Limited.

ISBN 978-1-7394-5044-1

Printed in Great Britain
To find out more about our books and resources visit www.boskypublishing.com

WHERE WE LIVE IS... CREATIVE

ART AND CREATIVITY ALL AROUND THE UK

WRITTEN BY EMILY SHORE
ILLUSTRATED BY MARION LINDSAY

bosky

CONTENTS

Introduction   page 6

Chapter 1: Festivals   **page 10**

Festivals Activities   **page 18**

Chapter 2: Makers   **page 20**

Makers Activities   **page 28**

Chapter 3: Performance   **page 30**

Performance Activities   **page 38**

CONTENTS

Chapter 4: Art Outside   page 40

Art Outside Activities   page 48

Chapter 5: Creative Journeys   page 50

Creative Journeys Activities   page 58

Conclusion   page 60

Glossary   page 62

Acknowledgements   page 64

Fern's right. But being creative can look like lots of different things, not just singing. You might use music or colour, food or nature, or even your own body to make something special, fun or interesting. In fact, being creative is a bit like flying — it can take your thoughts and your feelings to all kinds of beautiful places.

> It's like when you sing your song, Bay — you create a sound and a tune that tells people something about you. It's yours and it's special to you, but when you let it out other people can enjoy it too.

> Aw thanks!

Many people choose to live in creative places because they can be exciting and surprising. Creative places can bring lots of people together to celebrate, to discover, to make something, or to feel something. For some people, being in a creative place helps them to let out some of the things that are inside them.

In this book, we will travel with Fern and Bay to discover some of the creative places around us. We will find out about lots of different ways to be a maker or an artist, and pick up some ideas along the way about how we can get creative with the people we know. Each chapter ends with a few activities for you to try out, wherever you live.

Here's a peek at where we're going...

Festivals
Some places are home to exciting festivals that happen every year. These are often a celebration of something that is special to that place or to the people who live there. Festivals are a beautiful way to bring lots of people together in one place to have fun and connect with each other.

Makers
Some places bring people together to imagine, design and make new things. This could be anything from **crafting** with their hands to **animating** the programmes we watch on TV. When we work together, we can often create something even more special because of all the different voices and ideas that have been poured into it.

Performances
Have you ever watched a show on a stage? The performers might share a story or a song, or entertain the **audience** with movement and music. There is a special connection between the performers and the audience as they create a live experience, in that moment, that might be different every time.

Art Outside

Art and creativity can be anywhere, just waiting to be discovered. You might be walking through a busy city and see a big, bright painting on the side of a building. Or you might stumble across some impressive **sculptures** in the park that someone has carved from wood or stone. Art outside can make people think and feel different things, depending on where it is and who you are.

Creative Journeys

Have you ever been lost in a maze? A creative pattern of hedges or trees can lead you through so many twists and turns that you completely lose your sense of direction! You might also have been on an art trail, following **murals**, sculptures or clever **riddles** that lead you from one place to the next. You might end up in a completely different place to where you started, or you might go on a journey in your imagination – without even moving your feet!

CHAPTER 1
FESTIVALS

WHY DO PEOPLE FIND FESTIVALS CREATIVE?

Imagine living in a place where everyone looks forward to a special festival every year. It must be so exciting to see the organisers getting it all ready, and to feel the buzz of excitement in the air as the date gets closer. Imagine all the people who have travelled from far and wide to come to where you live because they want to be part of this creative celebration.

There are lots of different types of festivals and they often focus on a **theme** that people want to celebrate or experience together. This might be different styles of music and **performance art**, a celebration of **culture** and **diversity**, a **religious** festival, or a chance to remember a person or event from history.

Whatever the focus of the festival, you can probably expect a feast for all five **senses**!

Look at this place. What can you...

...see? (colour, movement, people, performances, costumes)

...hear? (music, speeches, crowds, singing)

...touch? (costumes, crafts and competitions)

...taste? (different types of food and drink)

...smell? (hot food, smoke from fireworks, fresh air)

All of these are points of connection for people. Whoever you are, whatever your age and wherever you come from, you can share the experience of these **vivid sensory** moments at a festival.

Look at how people have dressed up to enjoy the festival.

I bet the music sounds amazing!

There are lots of ways to be creative at a festival, whether it's with face paints and costumes, stage performances, or making art together. There might even be exhibitions or competitions to enter.

Festivals only happen because people have creative ideas about how to bring everyone together and make it an event to remember! It's a joint effort, with lots of different people sharing their ideas or using their creative talents. There might be planners and performers, chefs or bakers, musicians, artists or costume designers. Can you think of any others?

There are people who decide what the festival is going to look, feel and sound like, and people who bring it to life. There are also people who create and share posters, flyers or video clips to encourage others to actually come!

Often, a festival will happen every year, and in the same place. This adds to the excitement because people can look forward to it and come back again and again. Over time, the event will change as new elements are added and new members of the **community** offer their ideas. The festival itself is a creative work of art that is always unfolding.

Have you seen music outdoors?

How many people were watching together?

Have you visited a festival?

Were there more people than in your family?

How big was the stage?

Did you sleep in a tent?

Were there more people than in your school?

We have been to...

A FESTIVAL!

Eisteddfod, Wales

Try to say Eisteddfod using these sounds: igh - stedth - vod.

THE POWER OF WORDS

Eisteddfod is a family festival that's held in a different part of Wales every year. It's a celebration of Welsh language and culture that has been happening for hundreds of years.

It started out with poetry and music competitions, but over time it has grown and changed, like a living thing. It now includes all kinds of events, activities and performances for the whole family, and is the biggest cultural festival in Europe.

Language is creative — we can enjoy the sound and meaning of words and stories. Can you work out what these Welsh words mean? The pictures are clues. What does it sound and feel like when you say these words out loud?

coedwig
(forest)

bara
(bread)

cerdd
(poem)

Cerdd is pronounced like this: care-th.

What other types of art can be inspired by words and language? These pictures are clues.

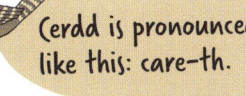

It's a song.

It's a collage.

CARNIVALS OF COLOUR

A carnival is like a street festival, where everyone's welcome! Carnivals are some of the most colourful and energetic outpourings of joy. They feel like a celebration of life, and of the cultures and communities that make up a particular place.

The sights, sounds and smells of a carnival all play a really important role in creating a delicious and lively experience, and there will often be a varied mixture of food and drink on offer. The parade can be one of the real high points of the event. Expect an explosion of **vibrant** costumes like nothing you've ever seen before, with steel drums, bells or shakers setting a rhythmic soundtrack. There are lots of different carnivals that happen around the UK, and many are completely free so anyone can just show up and share in the joy!

How many different types of material can you spot in this costume?

Why do you think people like to dress up for a carnival? Can you find every colour of the rainbow in this picture?

feathers
sequins
ribbons
buttons
scarves
face paints

MAKING MUSIC

Sharing music together is a great way of connecting with other people, having fun and enjoying yourself.

There are over 100 independent festivals that happen every year in different parts of the UK, and musical performances play a big part in these. Festivals often include entertainment, arts and crafts, and the chance to learn new skills, as well as some incredible performances. Can you think of a time when you made a friend while you were doing something creative together or trying something new?

As well as the musicians and artists, there are creative teams who design and organise each festival, and plenty of volunteers. These are the people who give their time to make safe and fun spaces for everyone and keep festivals running smoothly.

If you were helping to organise a festival, why might you need to use some creative problem-solving? Can you think of any examples?

That looks complicated. There's a stage, lights, and instruments. And a sound desk, speakers and microphones. And then everyone will need food, drink and toilets. There's a lot to organise!

Imagine singing with other birds from all over the world, Fern...

oh yes, I'd love to hear their songs!

SHARING BETWEEN NATIONS

Some festivals are an invitation for people from all over the world to come together through creativity. International festivals like these happen across the UK, from Scotland in the north to the Isle of Wight, which is an island in the south.

They are a **global** celebration of things like music, dance, **opera** and theatre performances, art and books from around the world. These festivals encourage people from different countries and backgrounds to share thoughts and ideas. Sometimes a festival will have a theme that brings all of the different performances or works of art together. It's amazing to see how each one presents the same theme but in its own **unique** way.

Why do you think the performing arts can help people from different parts of the world to connect and understand each other?

FESTIVALS OF LIGHT

Diwali is a very important festival in Indian culture and has become one of the most famous festivals of light across the world. It is a joyful celebration of new beginnings, of good defeating evil and of light winning over darkness.

Thanks to the growing community of **Hindus** and **Sikhs** in Leicester, the city's celebrations are some of the biggest outside of India.

The Golden Mile glows with brightly coloured Diwali lights, and the brilliant Wheel of Light invites people to enjoy the view from up high. This kicks off two weeks of creative events and family fun in the community, including dance performances, street art and a lantern procession by local school children.

Light can be used in so many creative ways to bring a community together in celebration.

Wow, this looks magnificent!

Diwali Celebrations on Leicester's 'Golden Mile'

Get Creative At Home

ACTIVITY

PAPERCHAIN POEM

Create your own paperchain poem with your friends by being a creative team. Teamwork makes the dream work!

Collect ideas together for your paperchain poem

Choose what you want your poem to be about and then you can each write your own thought or sentence on a strip of paper. How about adding patterns and drawings too? This will make everyone's paper strip unique, and will create a beautiful chain when they all come together.

Join the strips of paper by starting with one strip and sticking the ends together to make a loop. Then add another strip by pushing one end through the first loop and sticking the ends together to create your second loop. When you have joined lots of them, your loops turn into a chain.

Make sure to hang your poem somewhere where other people can enjoy it. You could even read each sentence out loud to make it into a performance!

Here are some ideas for topics to get you started:

Our favourite things about nature
Start the sentences with 'My favourite thing in nature is…'

The happiness connection
Start the sentences with 'One thing that makes me happy is…'

When I am brave
On the outside of the strip of paper, start the sentences with 'On the outside, I look…' On the inside of each strip, start the sentences with 'On the inside, I say to myself…'

Or you can come up with your own ideas!

ACTIVITY

My Musical Home Loops

Use pieces of paper to arrange your musical home loops

How many things can you find around your house that could be used as a musical instrument? Here are some ideas:

- Tap a biscuit tin with a wooden spoon.
- Fill drinking glasses with different amounts of water and then tap them gently with a spoon to make different notes.
- Close the Velcro on a shoe (and open it again!).
- Rustle some tissue paper or a piece of wrapping paper.
- Crunch an ice-cream cone into a bowl (when you're finished, you can eat this up!).
- Stir a bowl of rice with a chopstick.
- Press a clicker on the end of a pen.
- Twist a salt shaker. (Did you know that some people call these salt mills?)
- Tap a metal water bottle with a pencil.
- Drop a metal spoon on a coaster. (This works really well with a ceramic coaster!)

Making loops

Put five of your things in a row to make your own music.

A good way to start is to make each sound four times and then move onto the next sound.

If you are making your loop with a friend, you can take it in turns. Person 1 makes a sound four times, then person 2 makes a sound four times. Keep going and see what music and patterns you can make!

CHAPTER 2
MAKERS

HOW MANY DIFFERENT WAYS ARE THERE TO BE CREATIVE BY MAKING THINGS?

Making is exciting. You can make with your hands, with your voice, with tools and machines, with computers, with light and sound, and even with food and plants. We are all makers, even if we don't realise it.

Sometimes, you might plan what you're going to make before you start. You might draw a sketch or work out what steps you need to take, and then follow the instructions. Other times, you might just go for it and see what happens! You may be happy with it first time, or you can have another go and make some changes. Learning something from each try is a very important part of the creative process.

However you do it, when you make something it can feel a bit like putting a little part of yourself out into the world. When people look at it, enjoy it or use it in some way, they are connecting with you and your creativity.

Have you ever worked with a partner or a group of people to make something? This can be extra exciting because you end up using lots of different thoughts and ideas to shape whatever you make, and when it's finished it might be very different to whatever you could have imagined all on your own. But it can also be difficult because you might not all agree on exactly what you want to make, or how it should look.

Often, lots of different makers choose to come together in one place to share ideas because they feel that it fires up their own creative energy. Makers are often very good at celebrating each other's creations and encouraging more people to get making. These creative communities are also a fun place to feel challenged and stretched, so that you push yourself to experiment. There is a freedom to try new things, to learn lessons, and to do things a little differently next time.

It is important to remember that we all have our own thoughts and feelings about whether something is good, or beautiful, or interesting. When lots of makers gather together, there is usually a good understanding that we are all different and special, so the things we make will all be different and special in their own ways too.

Backstage at a Fashion Show

The first time I made a nest, I had to start all over again three times! But the last one was beautiful, and really strong too.

21

Have you made something before? Your own unique creation!

How big was your craft?

Have you ever been taught how to make something by someone in your family or a teacher?

Did you use drawing, painting, joining different materials, paper, knitting or crocheting by making knots with wool?

We have...

CREATED SOMETHING!

I like creating as it makes me calm.
Imogen, aged 6

I like being creative because you can do what you want – you don't have to copy a particular thing.
Maya, aged 6

LOOKING TO THE FUTURE

There is an area of Salford that looks and sounds a bit like a city from the future. It has been designed and built to be a place where creative people come together to dream up new ideas.

Today, the people who make things together at Salford Quays are often thinking about TV programmes, film, video games, computer programmes, and all of the ways that we might be able to use these types of technology that we haven't even thought of yet. Some of these makers are huge companies and others are small groups of people who are just starting to work out how they could turn their ideas into something real. With all of these creative minds whirring around each other, the whole place seems to fizz with its own special energy.

The quays are connected by canals all the way to the sea!

Salford Quays

ALL FIRED UP

People have been making pottery in Stoke-on-Trent for over 300 years! Today, you can visit many factories, museums, galleries and shops that celebrate the history and tradition of this craft.

The soft clay is shaped with hands or tools and then fired in a very hot oven called a kiln so that it hardens and keeps its shape.

Next comes more creative design work as the pottery is painted.

Many of the mugs, bowls, jugs and pots that we use every day have been made this way.

The Potteries bring together art and design (ideas about how you want something to look, like which shapes and colours to use) with business, industry and invention (the creative work of making something with your hands, or with machines, thinking about how the actual making process could be better, and then selling what you've made!).

Some of the tools and the processes have developed over time, and the many different creative minds working together at the Potteries have challenged each other to experiment with new ways of doing things.

Why is there such a young child in the factory?

A long time ago, many children as young as six years old were paid a very small amount to do jobs at the Potteries, like carrying materials around. This was dangerous and unfair. It is a good reminder that one person's creative business shouldn't harm someone else.

Middleport Pottery, Stoke-on-Trent

Scrap Carriers, 1910

GETTING CRAFTY TOGETHER

Craft festivals are a celebration of creative people or small businesses that each have their own sense of style and design. These makers are usually people who get a lot of joy from creating things, and the crafts can include anything from birthday cards, candles and wall art to jewellery, clothing and pottery.

A big part of the joy and satisfaction of making something is to share it with other people, and craft fairs also give visitors a chance to try designing or crafting at creative workshops.

One of the most famous and popular craft festivals in the UK started in Bovey Tracey in Devon, and then moved to Cardiff in Wales, too, bringing together 150 makers of all kinds — that's a lot of making!

A craft market in Belfast

WHEN CREATIVITY COMES ALIVE

Flowers might look pretty and smell nice, but there's a lot more to them than that! Every year, there are lots of different flower and garden shows that take place in the UK, giving people a chance to express their creativity through planting and pruning.

The oldest is in Taunton and started about 200 years ago. At a flower show, different teams of people create gardens in very small spaces. They put together living displays, using flowers, trees, vegetables and herbs in new and eye-catching ways.

Judges award gold, silver and bronze medals to the gardens and displays that they think are most creative, interesting, bold, beautiful or like something they have never seen before. Sometimes, there are also extra awards, like certificates for the best displays by young gardeners, and awards for gardens that focus on learning and **scientific discovery**.

Topiary at Tatton Park, Cheshire

Look how creative you can be with plants and trees! Making a shape like these is called topiary. Try saying 'toe' - 'pea' - 'ary'!

ALL DRESSED UP

Some people let their creativity out by experimenting with the clothes we wear. Many people learn about fashion at universities and colleges in the UK, and there is a famous fashion event in London that happens twice a year.

At fashion shows, designers share their new ideas about materials, colours, shapes and styles. They draw their designs and then work with a team to turn these into clothes that can be presented at the show. They will choose someone to model their designs, walking up and down on a stage and showing them off from every angle. Photos will be shared all around the world, with people excited to see the latest fashion creations.

It's a chance for designers to throw their most bold and unique clothing ideas out into the world and to see what others think, so you will often see some very interesting and unusual looks!

Both photos: Manchester Metropolitan University Graduate Show, 2024

What do you think about this jacket?

It's all about confidence! If you feel good, you look good.

Get Creative At Home

ACTIVITY
MINI GARDEN DESIGNERS

Make your own mini garden, either by yourself or by working as a team. This is a great way to re-use things that might normally be thrown away. You can make gardens in ice cream tubs or lids, in old plates or bowls.

- Choose your holder and check with your grown up that it is okay to use.
- Add some stones first, and then some soil on top.
- Then find some moss to add some green to your garden.
- You can add plants or stones and you can create your own models too. Try making a little house with recycled cardboard packets. You could add mini bunting or small toy people.

Uplevel your garden

Add an extra level to your garden to make it more interesting. You could use some kind of stand to make the garden higher off the ground – try turning a metal lampshade frame upside down.

Here are some ideas for things to plant during the different seasons of the year. These ones are normally happy being planted in pots.

Spring: Try planting seeds after the frost has finished, in April or May. Marigolds have beautiful orange flowers. Cornflowers are blue.

Summer: Try planting strawberry plants or lavender in early summer. Both of these plants like sunny spots.

Autumn: Try planting Bellis seeds in September if you have a sheltered spot or a greenhouse.

Winter: Try adding mini daffodil bulbs (sometimes called dwarf narcissus or 'tête-à-tête') in November.

ACTIVITY

HOPE-FILLED, WOOL-WRAPPED STARS

- Cut some long strips of card — you could use empty cartons from home.
- Stick two or three strips together with glue to make a strong piece of card.
- When you have done this a few times and have four strong pieces, place them on top of each other in the shape of a star pattern.
- Tape the middle, where the strips join, to keep your star together.

- Use wool to tie a knot around the middle of the star. Then wrap the wool tightly around one of the pieces of card. When you are at the end of the card, stick the end of the wool to the card with tape.

- Do this again with more wool on each of the 'arms' of the star. If you want different options, you can try ribbon or long strips of fabric to wrap around the card. You might want to mix and match different colours and textures.
- If you are making a star at the start of a new year, you can hide a little piece of card underneath your wool. Write something that you hope will happen in the next year or a dream!
- When you have finished covering all of the star, hang it somewhere to make your room beautiful.

Tape your star together. Then wrap your wool.

CHAPTER 3
PERFORMANCE

WHAT'S SPECIAL ABOUT CREATIVE PERFORMANCES?

The thing about performances is that you never know exactly what's going to happen. Even though the performers and the stage team will probably plan and practise the show many times before they do it in front of an audience, every time they perform it to a group of people it's going to be slightly different. That's because it's being created live, there and then, in front of our eyes.

There is a special connection between the performers and the audience, which makes it different to watching TV or film on a screen. In a way, the audience is part of creating the performance on that day because we bring our own energy and emotions to it, and the performers can feel that on stage. We all share in it together, creating a one-off experience that can never be repeated in the exact same way.

The audience might laugh, gasp, cry or clap in different places, for example. Or something might go slightly wrong on stage and the performers have to think quickly to work around it. The last few minutes before the curtains open or the lights go down can often feel really exciting because once the show starts, anything could happen.

Performances are about entertaining the audience, but they also usually aim to make us feel something or to leave us with something to think about. Most performances will tell some sort of story, even if there's no speaking involved — music, dance and even telling jokes can all be a type of storytelling as the performers take the audience on a journey with them.

Often a performance will happen on a stage in a theatre. But this isn't always the case. Performances can happen in schools, in cafes or libraries, in homes or gardens, in fields or car parks — anywhere at all. And you don't need a big audience. Some people will perform in front of just one or two others, and some will perform in front of thousands.

Have you been in a show?

What type of creativity was in it?

Did you watch or did you perform?

How did you feel?

We have been to...

I love dancing because it makes me happy.
Elodie, aged 6

It was absolutely brilliant. I loved the music and the acting, but especially the music. It made me feel happy everywhere. I want to make my singing and dancing as good as that when I'm in a show.
Nathan, aged 8, went to see a musical in Manchester

What a beautiful day to see some shows!

FREEDOM ON THE FRINGE

Every summer, the streets of Edinburgh in Scotland are jam-packed full of visitors who have come to enjoy the world's biggest festival of performances. It's called the Edinburgh Festival Fringe because it happens around the edges — or fringes — of the Edinburgh International Festival.

The most exciting thing about the Fringe is that anyone can take part, with any type of performance, so it is a brilliant example of being completely free with your creativity.

There are children's shows, musicals and dance, and lots of comedy. It is an open invitation to performers to try new things in front of an audience and find out whether people enjoy it — you don't know until you try!

DRUMMING AND STRUMMING

Musical performances can be loud, energetic and exciting, or peaceful and relaxing. They can get people singing and dancing, or make people think and feel things in their own hearts as they listen.

There might be a mixture of instruments and voices, or just one performer. One of the beautiful things about music is that different groups of people from all over the world have created their own styles of music, and even their own instruments.

Irish **folk music** is a great example of a style of music that is strongly tied to a particular community of people and tells the story of their history. Local Irish pubs are well known for folk music performances that bring people together, using traditional instruments, rhythms and **melodies**.

How do people make a noise from these instruments?

Well, some are blown, some are plucked with your fingers and some are hit or shaken. Can you spot which ones?

MOVING TO THE MUSIC

Did you know that some storytelling happens without anyone saying a single word? Dance performances use music and movement to present a story to the audience. The dancers act out their parts using their bodies and faces to show what's happening and how they are feeling.

Along with the music, this tells the audience the whole story. Some very famous tales have been turned into ballet performances, including Swan Lake.

Northern Ballet in Leeds is a dance company on a mission to take their ballet shows to all audiences, so that everyone can enjoy this special type of storytelling.

I wonder who is birdwatching in the ballet?

Can you see the H and G on Hansel and Gretel's t-shirts? They look very happy.

Hansel and Gretel at the Northern Ballet, Leeds.

SPEAKING UP

When a poem is read or spoken out loud to an audience, this is called a spoken word performance. It's not just about the words on the page, but how they are presented or delivered to the audience.

The rhythm and tone of voice are important for getting a message across. Some spoken word events focus on one theme or message. Performers might speak up to support or celebrate something, or to protest against something. Inviting voices from a particular background or culture gives people a platform to share their experiences and points of view, especially if they have been silenced or overlooked in the past.

Free spoken word workshops and events, like Primary Voices Enfield, give primary school students a chance to proudly speak about what is important to them. The only expectation is that "you give everything a try in the workshops and that you don't talk negatively to discourage yourself before you share your magnificent words!"

I like the sound of performance poetry because wings make it very hard to write!

LETTING PUPPETS DO THE TALKING

When you think of puppets, maybe you picture a glove puppet that slips over your hand. But puppets can come in all shapes and sizes, and in all kinds of materials. They can be moved and controlled in many different ways and are often an exciting way to tell a story, teach a lesson, or send a message.

The puppet is so detailed!

PuppetSoup is a puppetry theatre company based in London and Wales, and their motto is 'Puppetry for everyone'. That's because they believe in using puppets in creative ways for all kinds of performances that anyone and everyone can enjoy – they don't even have to use words. They tour all over the UK, visiting schools, community groups, and even the Edinburgh Fringe festival, to share this special type of performance art through shows and workshops. There is a long history and tradition of using puppets in performances, but the artists also get a lot of fresh and creative ideas when they share their puppetry with new, young audiences.

Puppet created by PuppetSoup

Can you see how the puppeteer blends into the background? Your eyes focus on the puppet and you don't notice the hands much. It's so clever.

Get Creative At Home

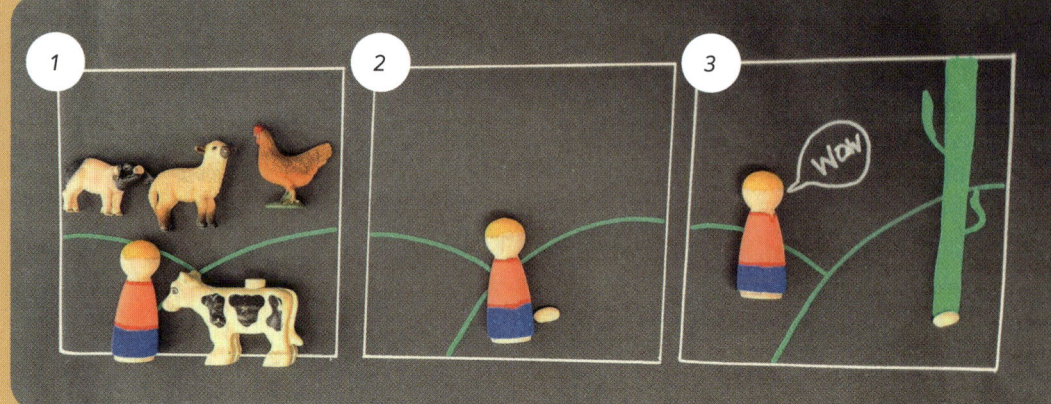

Think about your story's three parts

ACTIVITY
STORY ACTIONS

Can you tell a story to someone without using any words? Choose a story that you know well and use your body and props to act it out.

Props are things that you hold, wear or use to tell the story: for example, Cinderella might need a duster or a broom.

Act each part out but without any words, so you are only thinking about how you move and what the person in the story is doing.

See if the person watching can guess what the story is!

If you haven't done this before, it's a good idea to think about three parts of the story to act out:

1. **What happens at the start?**
   (e.g. Jack takes his cow to market)

2. **What happens in the middle?**
   (e.g. Jack swaps his cow for a bean)

3. **What happens at the end?**
   (e.g. Jack plants the bean and it magically grows)

ACTIVITY

PUPPET TALES

Make finger puppets or stick puppets to tell your story instead.

Try using paper or card to draw your person and add a lollipop stick that you can hold to control the puppet. You can even print out a picture and stick it onto card. You need to fix the lollipop stick to the back of your character.

Try making a simple mini theatre background out of a cardboard box. Draw a picture on the back of the cardboard box to set the scene.

Act out the stories for an audience using your puppets (remember your start, middle and end!).

Lolly stick puppets

ACTIVITY

KEEP THE WORDS IN YOUR HEAD! (MEMORY CHALLENGE)

Can you memorise a short poem and then speak it out loud to your friends or your family?

It could be the words from a rhyme that you know or a favourite song. Think about how you use your voice to speak. Can you make it exciting, interesting, sad, happy?

CHAPTER 4
ART OUTSIDE

WHY DO PEOPLE ENJOY ART OUTDOORS?

One of the really exciting things about art is that you can find it anywhere. You don't have to be in an art gallery or a museum, and it doesn't have to be displayed in a picture frame or on a stage. Some artists choose to create art in outside spaces because they want anyone and everyone to be able to enjoy or experience it.

Even the weather and the time of day will make a huge difference to the look and feel of the art — a sculpture might look bright and beautiful in the sunshine, but it might feel more gloomy in the rain, or even a little scary at night. Nature also plays its part in actually creating and changing the art over time. Wind, rain and seawater can wear away at some

Look at this sculpture!

A sculpture in Yarrow Valley Park, Chorley

materials so that they look very different after a few years of being outside in all seasons. Living plants and creatures can also affect art outside in different ways, changing what it looks like and how people feel when they see it. Small animals or birds might even make their homes in and around sculptures.

Art outside is sometimes strongly connected to its particular location and the artist has deliberately designed it to go in that very place. But sometimes it is a reflection of something that we can all connect with through our shared experience of being human and living on the Earth.

Have you seen art outdoors?

Was it a sculpture?

Can you guess how big it was? Maybe it was as big as a bus or smaller like the size of a bike.

Was it a painting or a mural?

Have you ever made your own art outdoors?

We have seen...

ART OUTDOORS!

> **I like seeing creative things and thinking, 'Wow! I wonder how they did that?' It gives me ideas for things to make.**
> *Millie, aged 6*

THE ARTIST, THE SUN AND THE SEA

When you first arrive at Crosby beach you might wonder why there are a lot of men along the shore, standing very still and gazing out to sea. But as you get closer, you will find that these men are actually life-size statues, or sculptures, made out of iron.

The sculptures are called 'Another Place'. There are 100 figures in total, with some of them standing on the beach and some further out in the water. They all seem to be looking out towards the horizon, watching and waiting.

Because they are outside, the effect of the sculptures changes — as the tide comes in and goes out, and as the sun rises and sets they look very different. The seawater and creatures also have an impact on the iron over time. Can you see how nature is partnering with the artist to create this work of art?

What do you think they're waiting for?

Each one of these sculptures weighs about the same as a fully grown male polar bear!

Another Place, Crosby by Antony Gormley

POWER & DRAMA, DAY OR NIGHT

Around the UK, there are some huge sculptures that are incredibly impressive and impossible to miss. You might even see some from the motorway as you drive past.

This is one of the Sperrins Giants that are found in Northern Ireland, in Omagh and County Tyrone. There are old stone circles that have been there for hundreds of years, and people tell **myths** about giants in the area. Now, there are three sculptures by Thomas Dambo. These are called Nowanois: The Storytellers, Darach: The Guardian, and Ceoldán: The Stargazer. The giants represent a connection to the beautiful area of the Sperrins — one points to the past, one to the present, and one looks to the future.

They are a beautiful and breathtaking giant-sized work of art, but also a celebration of reusing materials and **technology** — Thomas Dambo used leftover wood from Danish furniture-makers in his designs.

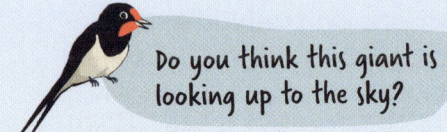

Do you think this giant is looking up to the sky?

Yes, this is Ceoldán who is looking at the stars and looking to the future.

Ceoldán: The Stargazer, Omagh by Thomas Dambo

ART AT THE HEART OF COMMUNITY

Painting Murals

In a very normal street of shops and houses, a local street artist might transform a bare brick wall with a **portrait** of a famous face. It will usually be someone who grew up in that area or has a connection to that community. These paintings can be really lifelike and striking, though they are usually many times bigger than life-size!

This kind of art at the heart of a local community has a way of bringing people together because they all feel that it's theirs and that they share it. It's often a portrait of someone who has achieved a lot of success — maybe an actor or a sportsperson — or someone who has used their skills or their voice to make good changes in the world. The artwork then becomes a powerful reminder and inspiration to the people who live around it that they, too, can do big things.

Artists Celebrating Artists

Sometimes, an artist wants to celebrate the creative work of someone else who has inspired them. We are all creative in different ways, and there is something special about using your own creativity to shine a spotlight on someone else's very different gifts and talents.

This is the story behind the huge scallop shell sculpture that you can visit on a beach near Aldeburgh.

It's one of those shells that can open up into two halves, but it's made of steel and is taller than a fully grown elephant!

The artist created it as a celebration of a musical composer called Benjamin Britten who used to live in this place. She wanted to create something solid and long-lasting, inspired by his musical talents.

Scallop, Aldeburgh by Maggi Hambling

Don't go too close! It's art! That's the problem with art outside — people and birds and animals might mess it up.

In fact, the artist wanted people to climb and sit on it, or use it as a shelter from the sun or rain. She said it wouldn't be completely finished until people connected with it like this.

PROTECTING THE UNDERWATER WORLD

Hannah Horn inking artwork

There is so much wildlife under the water that many people never see, including some species and habitats that have to be specially protected because they are at risk from pollution and climate change.

Hampshire & Isle of Wight Wildlife Trust, on the south coast, asked a local artist to paint six underwater scenes onto large wooden boards, and they connect together to bring a whole underwater world to life.

The artist used lots of different effects, including some shiny metallic paints, to show how beautiful and precious these creatures are — even if we can't see them for ourselves. She hoped that the murals would inspire people to find out more about the wildlife in these waters, and to do what they can to protect it.

Can you spot any really interesting or unusual sea creatures in the mural?

Look at those shiny scales!

Those rays look like they're flying!

Completed murals with artist Hannah Horn

Get Creative At Home

ACTIVITY

Nature Weaving

Can you weave together some objects from nature to make a mini nature fabric?

Collect together some sticks that have fallen to the ground, or long pieces of grass or plants when they have finished flowering in the autumn. Whatever you have in your collection, it needs to be bendy! Check with a grown up before you cut anything.

Put some sticks out in a row, a bit like a ladder, on the ground or on a tabletop. Then take your bendy grass or leaves and weave them together. That means you go under one stick and then over the next. You keep going under and over until you have got to the end of the row of sticks.

Take another stem of grass or a long, bendy leaf and start with the opposite action, so this time you go over the first stick and under the next one.

Keep going with more pieces to build up your weaving.

ACTIVITY

PATTERNS IN THE PARK

You can also try making a nature picture on the ground. Gather things like sticks, feathers, leaves, fallen petals and stones and arrange them into a picture or pattern. Think about using different colours and textures.

Use litter pickers or gloves to gather up rubbish in your local park. <u>Always</u> check with your grown up that it is safe to collect because some rubbish can be dangerous or very dirty. Arrange your collection into a picture or montage on the floor (but don't touch the rubbish with your hands, use the litter pickers!). Take a photo! Then, using your litter pickers, put all the rubbish in a bin.

ACTIVITY

BARK RUBBINGS

It's quick and easy to create different patterns by making bark rubbings.

Take a piece of paper and hold it flat against the trunk of a tree.

Try to keep the paper still. Using a wax crayon on its side, gently rub the crayon across the paper.

Go over the different parts of your paper two or three times. Little by little, the wax crayon will start to show the pattern from the tree trunk but on your paper. This is called a rubbing.

CHAPTER 5
JOURNEYS

HOW CAN CREATIVE ART TAKE YOU ON A JOURNEY?

Some journeys are about getting from a starting point to an end point. You move from one place to somewhere different. Often, you will follow a map or a plan, or some kind of instructions.

When you go on a creative journey, you might not have an actual map but you will have something to guide you. This might be a clear path in front of you, or it could be pictures or clues that lead you on from one point to the next. Think about how a maze invites you into a puzzle, or a woodland trail gives you things to look out for along the way.

Some journeys are more about how you think and feel than where you actually travel and end up. Even if you finish exactly where you started, you might have been on a journey in your heart and in your head. You might feel differently at the end to when you started — more **inspired**, more calm and peaceful, more excited. You might have learned something along the way, or seen something that you've never seen before, or just had a lot of fun!

A creative journey might be fast and energetic (like a frantic treasure hunt), or it might be slower and more thoughtful

My wings are getting a little tired, but my head is buzzing with things to try out when we get home...

(like a walk around the paths of a **labyrinth**). It's often more important to think about what you're seeing and experiencing on the journey than just to focus on getting to the end.

Some artists group together to create a trail or journey that includes all of their different styles, crafts and ways of working. These kinds of journeys can be really interesting and inspiring because they show so many different personalities and creative ideas.

One of the really exciting things about creative journeys is that they will never be the same twice. Even if you go back to exactly the same place and follow exactly the same path, your thoughts, feelings and experience of the journey will be different every time. It depends how you're feeling that day, what the weather's like, who's coming with you on the journey, and a hundred other things!

We've been on our own journey as we've discovered so many places around the UK that are creative in all kinds of different ways! Do you feel like you've learned some things that you didn't know before we started, and even got some new ideas to try out for yourself?

Have you followed a trail?

Were there a lot of things to see?

Did you have a map?

Where was the trail – outdoors, in a city, near the coast, in a forest?

We have been on...

AN ART TRAIL!

> '[A trail] feels like stepping into a story. There are massive slides, twisty wooden houses up in the trees, and places to climb and explore. It's not like a normal playground – it feels wild and magical, like you're in an adventure.'
>
> *Jacob, aged 9*

GET LOST!

A maze is like a big outdoor puzzle. It can be any shape or size, and the paths can be marked out with walls, hedges, hay bales or even rows of corn.

One of the most famous hedge mazes is at Hampton Court Palace, which used to be the home of King Henry VIII. It's also the oldest one in the country — more than 300 years old! It's called a puzzle maze because there are lots of places where you can take a wrong turn or run into a **dead end**. It usually takes people about 20 minutes to get from the outside to the middle, and then they have to find their way back out again!

It's so easy when you've got a bird's eye view. No, don't go that way!

The maze at Hampton Court Palace, London Borough of Richmond

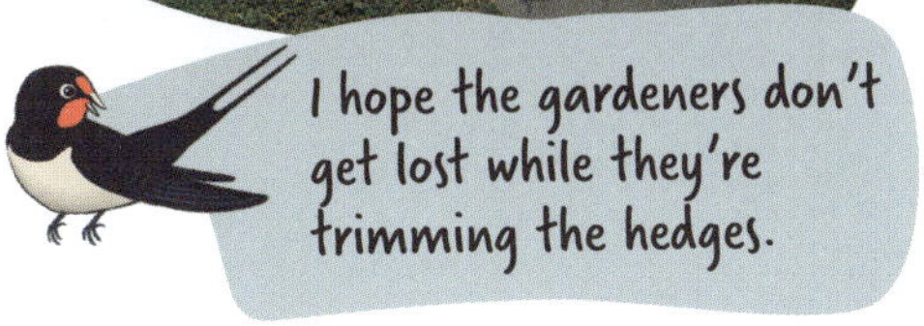

I hope the gardeners don't get lost while they're trimming the hedges.

PLAYFUL PITSTOPS

When you go for a walk in the woods, you probably don't expect to find yourself in a giant ants nest, a snake pit, or crossing a river of crocodiles...

But along a woodland trail, you can discover a different creative pitstop around almost every corner. That's because someone has put a lot of creative thought and energy into planning your journey through the woods.

Each stop on a trail, or each play area, has a theme to spark your imagination, like an enchanted wood or a giant's hand. The makers and artists have thought of lots of different ways for people to enjoy their creations.

Have you noticed that this sculpture is made from wood? This means that the hand blends in with the trees and you only realise what it is as you get closer.

The Giant Hand of Vyrnwy, Powys by Simon O'Rourke

Labyrinth at Fieldhead Hospital, Wakefield

A PEACEFUL PATH

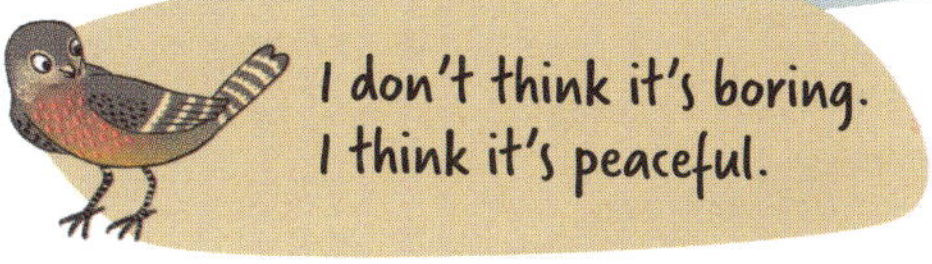

Isn't it a bit boring if you can't make any wrong turns?

I don't think it's boring. I think it's peaceful.

A labyrinth is a bit like a maze, but there is just one path to follow. It winds around, making lots of twists and turns, but it always leads to the middle.

It's not meant to be a puzzle or a game, like a maze. You're not meant to have to work it out. The idea is that it gives your body and your mind a few minutes to be calm and focused, to rest and to feel whatever you feel. If you follow the path, you can trust that you will make it to the centre. You just have to keep going.

You will sometimes find a labyrinth in the grounds of a hospital, like this one at Wakefield. If you're not very well, not very happy, or you're visiting someone you love at the hospital, you might have a lot of big feelings or worries. The labyrinth is a space for people to have some calm and peaceful time to themselves, focusing on putting one foot in front of the other.

Look — the doctors and nurses sometimes need a break too.

STACKING STONES

Have you ever hunted for stones on a beach? It's fun to choose the best ones – the smoothest or the most interesting colours and patterns – and to sort them into different shapes and sizes.

One artist, James Brunt, has taken this to a whole new level with his beach art on the Yorkshire coast. He has experimented with choosing and stacking stones in interesting and eye-catching ways, such as this wide circle of stones that gradually change from smallest to biggest.

It almost feels like a path, leading you round and upwards to the highest and largest stack. At this point, the path drops like a rollercoaster and you start again at the smallest pebbles.

It's such a simple idea, but it creates a feeling of growing excitement, anticipation, worry, or just energy as the stones build up – and then you're back in the calm and safety of the pebbles once again.

South Landing pebbles, Yorkshire by James Brunt

> Imagine how long it took James to find all of those stones! I wonder how far along the beach he had to go.

Alfred and Seth helping on La Boca mural

Murals tell the stories of towns and cities. They celebrate its history, industry and personality, and make people feel proud to live there.

A CITY TREASURE HUNT

You don't have to be at the beach, out in the countryside, in the woods or in the middle of nowhere to find yourself on a creative journey. In Leeds, one of the largest and busiest cities in the country, you can go on a creative treasure hunt as you try and spot all of the different murals that have been painted around the city centre.

Wherever you look, walls, buildings and bridges have been turned into huge and eye-catching works of art. There are so many different artistic styles to enjoy — detailed paintings that look so real that you can't believe your eyes, 3D illusions that seem to pop out of the wall, and abstract explosions of colours and shapes to brighten up the streets.

Get Creative At Home

ACTIVITY

SCAVENGER HUNT WALK

Draw a spotting trail map around the area where you live.

Draw the roads and colourful arrows to show which way to go.

What are five interesting things to look out for on the way? Draw pictures of them in the right places on your trail map. It could be a big tree or a corner shop or a bus stop.

Draw a checkbox next to each thing to spot.

See if a friend or family member can follow your trail. Do they end up somewhere different or back where they started?

Always make sure you stay safe by keeping to pavements and walking with your grown up. And if you want to try it again and make it trickier, you can add more things to look out for.

ACTIVITY
NATURE MAZE

Make a maze in the garden or park using things like sticks, stones and leaves and see whether a friend can follow it to the middle.

- Place the stones, sticks or leaves in two lines to make a path. (Top tip: Don't do this on a windy day because your paths will get blown away!) You'll need to gather quite a lot of materials to make the edges of your paths.
- Remember to include some wrong turns and dead ends!
- Put something special in the middle to show that this is the goal.

If you want to make a smaller version, you could make a mini maze for one of your toys. Move the toy through the maze to find the way to the middle!

WHERE SHALL WE GO NEXT?

We have been all over the UK looking for creativity! Have a look around you. You might find some of these creative things near to your home.

Look for:

- Local festivals
- Art like paintings, murals and sculpture
- Trails taking you on a journey to find art or creativity
- Local authors who have written new stories
- Workshops with makers that will help you to be creative
- People creating different designs with lots of different materials or with plants or with clothes
- Performances with words, dancing or music

Wherever you live, it won't be far from something creative.

And you might want to be creative too!

Seth practising spray painting

Alfred and Seth watching Alex Curran painting a mural in Stockport

Do you feel inspired now, Bay?

Yes, I do actually. I've had an idea for a picture I would like to make. Maybe with twigs.

Can I join in? That sounds really fun.

Of course you can!

GLOSSARY

abstract A type of art that uses shapes and colours in interesting ways but isn't supposed to look like anything real.

animating Turning drawings or models into moving images, like a cartoon.

audience People who are watching or listening to a show, or enjoying the art that someone has created.

comedy A type of storytelling or performance that aims to make people laugh.

community A group of people who are connected in some way and have some things in common.

crafting Making things with your hands, and often with art supplies like glue, paints and other materials.

culture The ideas, beliefs, language, food, art and clothing styles shared by groups of people, often because they have grown up in a certain part of the world.

dead end A blocked path, so you have to turn back and choose a different way to go.

discourage Cause someone to lose confidence or enthusiasm.

diversity Variety, difference.

emotions Feelings

folk music A traditional style of music that tells stories of a particular culture or group of people.

global All around the world.

grants and donations Money that is given to support a particular group or activity that is seen to be doing good work.

Hindus People who follow the beliefs and teachings of the religion of Hinduism.

illusion Something that is confusing to look at so that your eyes struggle to make sense of it. For example, a picture that looks like one thing from a distance but, when you get close up, is actually something else.

inspired Excited by a new idea because of something that you have seen, heard or experienced.

labyrinth A path that twists and turns back on itself but eventually leads to the centre.

melodies Musical tunes.

mural A large picture that has been painted straight onto a wall.

myths Stories that have been passed down through history, often involving supernatural or mythical creatures.

opera Telling a story through music, singing and acting.

performance art Artwork that is created through people behaving in a certain way, with an audience either watching or being part of it.

portrait A photo, painting or drawing of a particular person.

protest To speak up or take action against something that you don't think is good, right or fair.

pruning Cutting back branches and twigs to keep plants looking neat and healthy.

religious Believing in a god or gods, and following the teachings and actions of a religion (like praying and celebrating special holidays).

riddle A question or short poem that has a puzzle in it, so you have to work out the answer.

scenery Painted sheets or boards on a stage to give a background to the show, or to give more information about where the performers are supposed to be. It can help to create an imaginary world and make the show more believable for the audience.

sculpture A piece of art that has been carved or modeled out of solid material.

scientific discovery Finding out more about the world, understanding how things work, and learning new ways of doing things.

senses Seeing, hearing, smelling, tasting and touching.

sensory Exciting for all of your different senses.

Sikhs People who follow the beliefs and teachings of the religion of Sikhism.

technology Using maths, science and machines to design and build things.

theme A subject or idea.

tone of voice The way that someone speaks, and not just the actual words they use. This includes how loudly or quickly they speak, and whether they sound angry, excited, sad or gentle, for example.

trading Buying and selling between people and between countries, or swapping one thing (that you don't need or that you have too much of) for something else (that you do need and don't have).

tradition Beliefs and ways of doing things that have been handed down from parents to their children, sometimes again and again over hundreds of years.

vibrant Lively, colourful and energetic.

vivid Bright, colourful, strong or striking.

ACKNOWLEDGEMENTS

With our utmost gratitude to the following artists and organisations, without whom our project would have been far less creative and wonderful.

CHAPTER 1: FESTIVALS

Page 7 Photograph: Sophie Macauley

Page 11 Photograph: Aranxa Esteve / Unsplash

Page 13 Photos thanks to and credit to Eisteddfod Genedlaethol Cymru | FfotoNant
Singing photograph by Sander Hallaste / Unsplash
Collage photograph by Andy Vult / Unsplash

Page 14 Photograph: Ugur Arpaci / Unsplash

Page 16 Photograph: Bozhin Karaivanov / Unsplash

Page 17 Diwali Celebrations on Leicester's 'Golden Mile', Photo with thanks to Visit Leicester
Photograph by Beth Walsh

CHAPTER 2: MAKERS

Page 21 Backstage at the Manchester Fashion Institute Show 2024, New Century, Manchester. Photography Richard Kelly, courtesy of Manchester Metropolitan University.

Page 25 Scrap Carriers image courtesy of The Potteries Museum & Art Gallery, Stoke-on-Trent
Photograph (Middleport Pottery): Public Domain
Photograph (Craft Fair): haoliang, Belfast, United Kingdom

Page 26 Photograph: JR Harris / Unsplash

Page 27 Designer Georgia Valentine, photography Richard Kelly, courtesy of Manchester Metropolitan University.
Designer Anna Leslie, photography Richard Kelly, courtesy of Manchester Metropolitan University.

CHAPTER 3: PERFORMANCE

Page 33 Photograph: Theo Felten

Page 35 Aerys Merrill and Albert González Orts in *Hansel & Gretel*, Northern Ballet. Photograph: Emily Nuttall

Page 36 Photograph: Freepik
Write2Speak are an organisation who offer a range of workshops and projects supporting young people and adults to express themselves through spoken word. Based in London, Write2Speak work across the UK. Enfield Primary Voices is an Art Council England funded project delivered by Write2Speak, working closely with 30 primary schools in Enfield.
write2speak.co.uk

Page 37 Photograph: PuppetSoup

CHAPTER 4: ART OUTSIDE

Page 41 Photograph: Andrew Hall / Unsplash

Page 43 Antony Gormley, Another Place, 1997. Cast iron.
100 elements: each 189 x 53 x 29 cm
Installation view, Crosby, Merseyside, UK. Photograph by Stephen White & Co. © the artist

Page 44 Thomas Dambo, Ceoldán, The Stargazer
Thomas Dambo has made more than 160 of his giant troll sculptures all over the world. All using recycled materials. See more of his work at www.thomasdambo.com
Photograph with thanks to F. Smith

Page 46 Maggi Hambling CBE, *Scallop*, 2003.
Stainless Steel, 4.1 x 4.6 x 2.45m
Aldeburgh Beach, Suffolk, England, UK
Photograph by Anna McCarthy ©
www.annamccarthy.com

Page 47 Hannah Horn
Artist Hannah Horn inking artwork © Sian Addison
Completed murals with artist Hannah Horn © Strong Island Media

Hampshire & Isle of Wight Wildlife Trust is committed to creating a wilder future by 2030, where nature is recovering, wildlife is returning, and ecosystems are being restored across our counties. With the support of more than 29,000 members, we want to see many more people on nature's side. We aim to engage 1 in 4 people, encouraging them to take action for nature by becoming part of Team Wilder.

CHAPTER 5: CREATIVE JOURNEYS

Page 53 The Maze, looking east, Hampton Court Palace
© Historic Royal Palaces. Photograph: Vivian Russell

Page 54 Simon O'Rourke
The Giant Hand of Vyrnwy was sculpted by Simon O'Rourke, and commissioned by the Forestry Commission Wales, now called Natural Resources Wales.
Photograph by Heather Sargeant

Page 56 Fieldhead Labyrinth, Fieldhead Hospital, Wakefield. Photograph © Deadline Digital
South Landing pebbles by James Brunt
Photograph © James Brunt

Pages 57, 60, 61 Photos: Sophie Macauley

Far from being the perfect fit for Peter O'Toole it occurred to him that the pair of them were better cast as Dick Dastardly and Muttley. He had plotted and connived with dastardly schemes, but it was Muttley who always saved the day. Perhaps they might do a film of their life story, the two of them would be perfect for it.

To Moriarty's surprise Nathan stopped and roared with laughter. He looked up at Nathan, pleased to hear him laugh for the first time in days. He then understood his lap sitting psychotherapy had done its work.

This walk had, to use that appalling Americanism, "given him some perspective." Nathan no longer needed to chase the role of Peter O'Toole. He was no longer haunted by the split personality within him. He had stopped being driven by the importance of being Peter. He realised he already was, and always would be, in some way Peter. That man was as much a part of him as his own skin, but he wasn't all of him. He was a facet. An element that when needed, could, and would come into play. He still did not fully understand how these fugue states worked, but decided not to think too deeply about it. It was probably just his deep familiarity with O'Toole, wasn't it? Or had he studied that man so intensely, for so long, that he had altered his own character?

In the bioscope of his mind the stutter of a film projector started up, a scene from Casino Royale flickered onto mental screen. Peter O'Toole stood on a wide oak stairway in full highland regalia with a set of bagpipes tucked under one lean arm. Below him stood Peter Sellers in a sharp sixties suit.

"Are you Richard Burton?" asked O'Toole.

Sellers joyfully called back, "No I'm Peter O'Toole."

The confident tones of O'Toole replied, "Then you sir, are the finest man who-ever lived." Those bright blue eyes turned and looked directly at Nathan. 'Don't worry old sport. Whenever you need me, I will be here.'

The vision faded. Nathan chuckled to himself. From now on he decided, whether he accepted the film role or not, he simply needed to focus on the importance of being Nathan.

Printed in Dunstable, United Kingdom